Teachin' Smart

Ideas to Make Teaching Easy, Efficient, and Fun!

Written by Linda Holliman

Editor: Alaska Hults

Illustrator: Ann Iosa

Project Director: Carolea Williams

CTP © 1999 Creative Teaching Press, Inc., Huntington Beach, CA 92649

Table of Contents • . .

Introduction   **4**

A is for . . .   **5**
(ABC Book Graphic Organizer, After-Christmas Tree, Albums, Alliteration Arranging, Alphabetical Order, Aprons)

B is for . . .   **7**
(Baby Wipes, Balloons, Balls, Barrettes, Big Book "Pockets," Birthdays, Blocks, Book Talk, Bookmarks, Border Fun, Bottled Ink Bingo Markers, Buttons)

C is for . . .   **11**
(Calculators, Calendar Pictures, Calendar Shapes, Candy, Cereal Boxes, Chalkboard Paint, Clay Colors, Clipboards, Clothes Hangers with Clips, Color Coding, Colorful Art, Crazy Containers)

D is for . . .   **15**
(Dating, Disk Holders, Divided Boxes, Do-It-Yourself Dry Erase Boards, Dog Bones, Dominos)

E is for . . .   **17**
(Easels, Egg Cartons, Eggs, Envelopes, Erasers)

F is for . . .   **19**
(Fabric, File Cabinet, File Folders, Flags and Banners, Flashlights, Flyswatters, Fold and Crease)

G is for . . .   **22**
(Garland, Gift Game, Glasses, Glue, Greeting Cards, Guest Reader)

H is for . . .   **25**
(Hallway, Hats, Hobby Hall, Horizontal Picture Holders, Hula Hoops)

I is for . . .   **26**
(Ice Cube Trays, Ideas, Instant Programs, Interactive Charts, Interesting Information)

J is for . . .   **28**
(Jars, Jewelry, Jigsaw Puzzle Pieces, Journals, Jump Ropes)

K is for . . .   **30**
(Kabob Cooking, Ketchup Week, Key Chains, Key Rack, Kool-Aid® Packages)

L is for . . .   **32**
(Lazy Susans, Letter Sorts, Letter Writing, Lima Beans, Luggage, Lumberyards, Lunch)

M is for . . .   **35**
(Magic Spray, Magic Tree, Magnetic Manipulatives, Marshmallow Number Stands, Master Planning, Menus, Metal Pails)

N is for . . .   37
(Name Necklaces, Napkin Rings, Nests, Newspapers, Noodles, Note Necklaces, Nuts)

O is for . . .   39
(Odds and Ends, Outrageous Outfits, Overalls, Overhead Projectors)

P is for . . .   41
(Paper-Cup Stacks and Lines, Paper-Plate Book Covers, Pencil Boxes, Picnic-Basket Center, Pillowcase Book Record, Place Mats, Pocket Chart, Poetry, Pointers, Pringles®-Can Tales, Print Shops, Project Boards)

Q is for . . .   45
(Question Quilts, Questions and Answers, Quill Pens, Quotation Marks)

R is for . . .   47
(Raffle, Read the Room, Restaurant Supply Store, Rocks, Round-Robin Sharing, Rubber Bands, Rulers, Rules)

S is for . . .   50
(Seating Charts, Seed Packets, Sewing Cards, Shaving Cream, Shoe Boxes and Bags, Silverware, Smiles, Stamping Kits, Stringing Blocks, Stuffed Animals, Swimming Pools)

T is for . . .   53
(Tables, Tackle Boxes, Tall Tales, Tape Recorders, Tents, Themes, Tic-Tac-Know, Tiles, Tin Cans, Tongue Depressors, Trays, Tubs)

U is for . . .   57
(Umbrellas, Unifix Cubes, U.S. Maps)

V is for . . .   58
(Very Important Person, Vinyl, Visors, Vocabulary Bookmarks)

W is for . . .   59
(WetSet™, Wheelbarrows and Wagons, Wikki Stix, Windows, Winter Picnics, Word Banks, Write the Room)

X is for . . .   61
(Xocoatl, Xylophones)

Y is for . . .   62
(Yarn, Year's End)

Z is for . . .   63
(Zone)

Reproducibles   64

Index   78

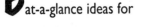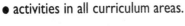
Introduction . . .

Add new life to your classroom and curriculum with *Teachin' Smart.* This book is filled with ideas to make teaching easier, more efficient, and loads of fun for teachers and children.

Because teaching today is more demanding than ever, you need a resource that offers instant, at-a-glance ideas for

- activities in all curriculum areas.
- organization.
- learning centers.
- student-work displays.
- behavior incentives.
- self-esteem builders.
- classroom decorating.
- arts and crafts.
- classroom management.

Teachin' Smart gives you all this and more. This resource saves you time and money by showing you how to use easy-to-find, everyday materials to enhance your curriculum and create an exciting, well-organized learning environment.

Organized in alphabetical order, the ideas presented in this book are easily referenced again and again, year after year. Reproducibles are included on pages 64–77 to make teacher preparation even easier and faster. In addition, an inspirational "word of advice" is presented for each letter of the alphabet to keep you motivated and focused on the important and rewarding career of teaching.

Children and parents will marvel at the ingenious ways you make learning meaningful and exciting when you use the ideas from this book. So get started today—it's simply *Teachin' Smart.*

A is for . . .

ABC Book Graphic Organizer

Choose two alphabet books about the same subject, such as insects, and read them aloud. Divide the class into pairs, and give each pair a photocopy of the ABC Ideas reproducibles (pages 64–66). Have children write the titles of the two books at the top of the appropriate columns and use the organizer to record ideas gathered from the two books. Use the organizer again and again with any two same-subject ABC books!

After-Christmas Tree

Start your bird unit after Christmas with an after-Christmas tree. Have a child donate an "un-dressed" Christmas tree (borrow his or her stand with the tree), and have the class decorate it with strings of popcorn and cranberries, peanut-butter and bird-seed pinecones, and other bird-friendly decorations. Set the tree outside your class windows, and create your own observation area. Have children keep a bird journal that includes drawings, observations, and other related information.

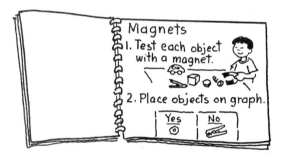

Albums

Photo albums with plastic page covers are a great place to store and protect learning-center activity directions. For young children, prepare rebus directions, and place them in large photo albums. For older children, prepare directions on index cards, and place them in smaller albums.

Alliteration Arranging

Read aloud an alliterative story, and then invite children to "arrange" their own alliterative sentences. Have each child choose a letter of the alphabet. Give each child half of a pad of small sticky notes. Have children write one word that begins with the letter they have chosen on each note. Ask children to spread out their notes on their desk to create an alliterative sentence. The beauty of using the sticky notes is that children do their own editing by moving the words around the desk before they write. Have children write and illustrate their sentences before placing them in a class book. Set up a reading center with books such as the following:

1000 Silly Sandwiches by Alan Benjamin
A My Name is Alice by Jane Bayer
Aster Aardvark's Alphabet Adventure by Steven Kellogg
Faint Frog's Feeling Feverish by Lillian Obligado
Where is Everybody? by Eve Merriam

A is for . . .

Alphabetical Order

Almost every supply can be organized in alphabetical order for easy reference. Obtain stacking containers with pullout drawers, one for each letter of the alphabet. (For "popular" letters, obtain two or more containers.) Alphabetize the supplies, and place each one in a drawer labeled with a letter. For example, place all balloons, buttons, beans, and bubbles in a *B* drawer. Remember to categorize items in a logical way so you will know where to look for them. For example, put all candy in a *C* drawer, rather than placing each kind in a separate drawer.

Aprons

Aprons with multiple pockets make great learning centers. Hang an apron over a chair, and use it to store books and materials for a learning center. To make an apron interactive, place self-stick Velcro on the outside center of each pocket. Choose a sorting activity, such as sorting shapes or beginning sounds. Make an index-card label for each sorting category, and attach a label to each pocket with Velcro. Have children sort objects or cards in the pockets.

A Word of Advice

ATTITUDE

Enthusiasm is contagious—and so is lack of it. —Anonymous

Attitude is one of a teacher's greatest tools in the classroom. As you try new ideas, materials, and techniques, remember that your attitude will be reflected in the attitude of your children.
If you're enthusiastic, your children will be, too!

is for . . .

Baby Wipes

Use baby wipes for cleaning desktops, chalk ledges, overhead transparencies, and sticky hands. They make the room smell good, too.

Balloons

Balloons are inexpensive, are readily available, and come in a variety of colors. Caution children to keep the balloons out of their mouths except when inflating them. Try these fun learning activities:

● Have groups of children blow up several high-quality balloons and use rubber cement to attach the balloons to make giant sculptures.

● Give each child a balloon. Read aloud *Alexander and the Terrible, Horrible, No Good, Very Bad Day* by Judith Viorst. Each time something terrible happens to Alexander, have children blow into their balloon once and hold it shut. By the end of the story, Alexander and the balloons will be ready to pop! Have children slowly deflate their balloon. Lead a discussion about feelings and positive ways to "let the air out of the balloon." Record children's responses on a large butcher-paper "balloon." When a child is having a bad day, have him or her refer to the balloon for ways to deal with his or her feelings. (You can use the balloon, too!)

● Cut small strips of paper, and write questions on them. Fold up each paper, and place it inside a balloon. Use a pump to blow up a balloon for each child. Have children take turns popping their balloon, reading the question, and answering it. Children wait their turn and listen to the questions in anticipation of the pop, so it's worth the noise.

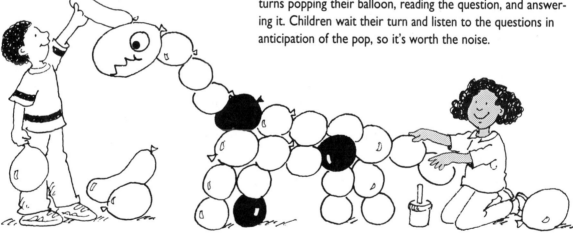

Balls

Use a large ball to represent hundreds, a medium-sized ball to represent tens, and a small ball to represent ones. Have three children stand in a row. One at a time, have children bounce their ball to indicate a number. Ask the class to write down the number "bounced." Check for correct responses. For informal assessment, say a number and have children bounce the ball the correct number of times.

is for . . .

Barrettes

Here's a cute idea for a learning center that provides children with the opportunity to practice the correct sequence of days of the week! Buy days-of-the-week barrettes at a discount or drug store. Draw a face on construction paper, and laminate it. Glue on "braids" made from yarn. Have children clip the barrettes on the braids in the correct sequence. You can also use metallic silver or gold permanent markers to label plain barrettes with the days of the week.

Big Book "Pockets"

Glue a large manila envelope to the inside back cover of a big book. Place sentence strips with sentences and words from the story in the envelope. Have children look through the book to find matches for each sentence and word on the strips. Or, challenge children to arrange the sentences on the strips in the order they appear in the book.

Birthdays

During the summer, write or stamp *Happy Birthday* on white lunch bags and add some decorations to make "birthday bags." Add a new pencil, stickers, a box of raisins or another snack package, and anything else appropriate for a birthday goodie. Store the bags in a "birthday box" and you are ready! Always make extra to allow for children who join your class. Celebrate summer birthdays as "half-birthdays." (June, July, and August birthdays are celebrated in December, January, and February.)

Blocks

Purchase blocks at a craft store for a language center, and try these activities:

● Invite children to use blocks to create simple sentences, practice alphabetical order, and identify parts of speech. Buy the largest blocks available and large round stickers. Write words on the stickers, and place one on each side of a block. Place stickers with new words on the blocks as children progress.
● Label each of three blocks *character*, *problem*, and *setting*. Write characters, problems, and settings on large round stickers, and place one on each side of the appropriate block. Encourage children to roll the blocks to help them generate story ideas.

B is for . . .

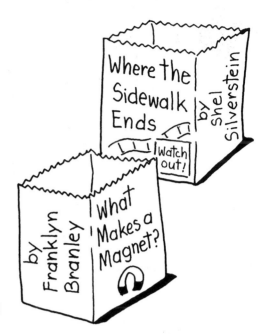

Book Talk

Give each child a white lunch bag, and have him or her write on the front and sides of the bag information about a book he or she has read (e.g., the title, the author, and an illustration of a favorite part of the story). On the back, have children write a summary of the book, including why they did or didn't like the story. While children work on their bags, pop some popcorn. Fill the bags, and have children meet in a circle to talk about their book and enjoy their snack. Give each child a chance to talk about what is on his or her bag, and invite the class to ask questions and discuss the stories. Don't forget to make one, too!

Bookmarks

Fold a 12" x 18" (30.5 cm x 46 cm) piece of construction paper lengthwise into thirds, and cut it apart at the folds to make three bookmarks. Make several bookmarks in this way. Have each child write his or her name on a bookmark and decorate it. Then, laminate each one. Place the bookmarks in a can at a classroom library/reading center. When children choose a book from a shelf or tub, have them place their own bookmark in the space so they know exactly where to return the book when they are finished.

Border Fun

Borders aren't just for bulletin boards anymore! Use strips and pieces of colorful borders in the following exciting ways:

- Cut apart borders with individual images to create math manipulatives, game pieces, and graph markers.
- Write directions on individual cut-apart border images for instant task cards.
- Use an ABC border to assess children's knowledge of beginning, middle, and ending sounds. Give each child an ABC border strip and a clothespin. Say a word or show a picture that has the beginning, middle, or ending sound of a letter on the strip. Have children clip the clothespin on the appropriate letter on the strip.
- Cut a border strip to fit around each child's head. Tape each strip into a closed loop to make a "crown."

B is for . . .

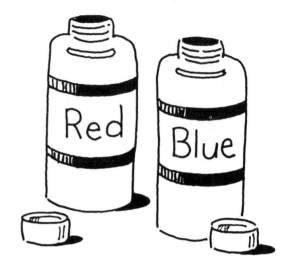

Bottled Ink Bingo Markers
Bingo markers are large round bottles of ink that make a bright circular stamp of color on the page. They are available in the school supplies section of most general stores. Have children use bingo markers to stamp patterns; combinations for specific numbers; and fact families for addition, subtraction, multiplication, or division.

Buttons
Fill a resealable plastic bag with 20 to 30 buttons for each child. Keep the buttons in a central location. Use buttons all year long for activities such as the following:
- For math, have children use buttons to practice sorting, patterning, and place value.
- To introduce or review adjectives, give each child a unique button and an index card. Have children list on the card as many adjectives as possible to describe their button. Place the index cards in a container, and place the container and buttons in a learning center. Have children visit the center to match buttons to their descriptions.

A Word of Advice

BLESSED

Blessed are the flexible for they shall not be bent out of shape! —Anonymous

Take each day one day at a time. Try to be flexible with your children.
They have their timetable and it doesn't always fit with our plans, the school day, or the weather!
Flexible teachers are open to possibilities, ready to take advantage of any opportunity to teach,
even if it presents itself as a praying mantis in the hands of a child.

C is for . . .

Calculators

Keep track of calculators by storing them in a hanging shoe organizer. Label each calculator and pocket with matching numbers. A missing calculator will be noticed at a glance!

Calendar Pictures

Use pictures from old calendars for the following center activities:

● Have children write descriptive paragraphs about the scenes or characters in the pictures.

● Have children write dialogue, including quotation marks, for two or more characters in the pictures.

● Give each child several pictures. Have children write captions for their pictures on index cards. Then, have children trade their pictures and captions with a partner, and challenge them to match the cards and pictures. The author gets a point for each correct match his or her partner makes.

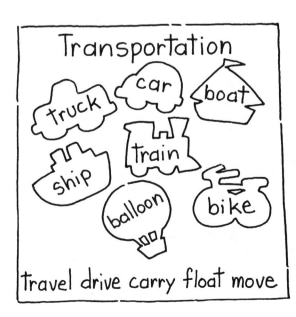

Calendar Shapes

Try the following ideas to get the most from your calendar shapes:

● Use the shapes as math manipulatives, game pieces, and task cards.

● For language arts, write a different word on each shape in a set, and have children use them for alphabetical order and grammar practice and syllable-sorting activities.

● For a writing center, display writing prompts on calendar shapes.

● Write thematic words on related calendar shapes, and display them as a word bank.

C is for . . .

Candy
Use candy throughout the year to make learning fun and sweet! Try these "tasty" ideas:
- Use seasonal candy, such as conversation hearts and Halloween candy, for sorting, patterning, and graphing activities.
- Obtain a bag of miniature jelly beans. Assign a monetary value to each color. Distribute a spoonful of jelly beans and a calculator to each child. Have children use the candy and calculators to make and solve addition, subtraction, multiplication, and division problems.
- Near Valentine's Day, give each child a small box of conversation hearts. Have children arrange their hearts on a piece of paper to create a story. Have children write words between the hearts to make complete sentences. Ask children to glue the hearts in place and read their story aloud to the class.
- Give children a candy that comes in assorted colors. Have children graph their candy by color. Provide children with graph paper to record their findings.

Cereal Boxes
Cereal boxes can be used for quick and easy learning-center activities like the following:
- Have children hunt for specific kinds of words on cereal boxes, such as words with short or long vowel sounds, words with blends, adjectives, or nouns.
- Have children write ingredients from one or more boxes in alphabetical order.
- Place task cards with comprehension questions in each box. Have children pull cards from a box, read the cereal boxes to find the answers to the questions, and record the answers on paper.

Chalkboard Paint
Turn any sturdy box, such as a photo box (available at craft stores), into a mobile chalkboard center. Spray-paint the lid with chalkboard paint and "season" according to the directions on the can. Store materials and supplies inside the box.

C is for . . .

Clay Colors

Obtain a class supply of red, blue, and yellow clay. Read aloud *Mouse Paint* by Ellen Stoll Walsh. Then, break the clay into small pieces, and give each child a chunk of each color. Ask children to break up each piece into several equal-size pieces. Invite children to choose two primary colors to mix together. Have children use crayons and the Colors reproducible (page 67) to record their results. Have children mix the primary colors to make orange, green, and purple. Then, invite children to mix secondary colors with primary colors to form new colors.

Clipboards

Clipboards are a must for the classroom. They provide a hard surface for writing and recording anywhere in and around the room. Use clipboards in the following activities:

- Clip a resealable plastic bag with materials, manipulatives, paper, and a pencil to each clipboard. Children can take the clipboards anywhere, use the materials in the bag, and have the hard surface for recording their information.
- Draw on the clipboards a graph or some other graphic organizer for children to use with the appropriate materials.

Clothes Hangers with Clips

Use clothes hangers with clips to hang and display big books, resealable plastic bags, pocket charts, bulletin board materials, and learning-center directions and supplies.

C is for . . .

Color Coding

Use green, black, and red markers to write a simple sentence on chart paper according to the following directions: Write the first letter of the sentence in green. Write the rest of the sentence in black. Write the ending punctuation in red. Point out that green means *go*, so a capital letter at the beginning of a sentence is written in green. Explain that red means *stop*, so the ending punctuation is written in red. For punctuation practice, have children color-code their sentences or use crayons to color parts of the beginning and end of sentences in activity books or on reproducibles.

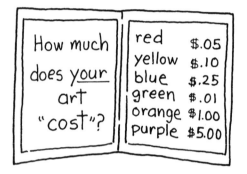

How much does your art "cost"?

red	$.05
yellow	$.10
blue	$.25
green	$.01
orange	$1.00
purple	$5.00

Colorful Art

Create this fun learning center to integrate money with art. Provide art materials and a chart that gives the color of each material a monetary value. After children complete their project (e.g., illustrate a scene from a book, paint a picture, or make a collage), have them make a list of all the colors they used and the monetary value you have assigned to each. Then, have children "add the colors" and record what it "cost" to create their piece.

Crazy Containers

It's time to look at containers in a new way! Turn a book bag, lunch box, purse, or hat box into a delightful container for classroom manipulatives, supplies, or center activities. Be sure to prepare containers to be used again and again. For example, measure the inside lid on a metal lunch box, and cut paper to fit it. Write activity directions or the box's contents on the paper, and laminate it. Use Velcro to attach the paper sign to the outside lid. When you are ready to use the box for another activity, make a new paper sign, and attach it in place of the old one.

A Word of Advice

CELEBRATE!

Each day comes bearing its gifts. Untie the ribbons! —Anonymous

Celebrations make learning fun and meaningful. Children love holidays and celebrations, so use them to your advantage. Besides popular celebrations, invite children to celebrate other special days, such as authors', artists', and scientists' birthdays; anniversaries of specific inventions or events; and fun "national" days, weeks, and months, such as National Smile Week or National Soup Month.

D is for . . .

Dating

Dating children's work should be so easy, but it isn't! Purchase date stamps at an office supply store, and place them in specific spots in the classroom. Children enjoy the official feel of stamping a date on their work. Assign a child to be in charge of changing the date each day, or make it a part of your calendar activities.

Disk Holders

Use computer-disk holders for three-ring binders to organize manipulatives such as small letters, words, and rebus pictures. Keep the disk holders in a binder with a "menu" of activities and recording sheets.

Divided Boxes

Store math and language-arts manipulatives in divided boxes from craft stores. Obtain boxes that are divided into several different-sized compartments to accommodate different-sized materials. To quickly make a math center, place several kinds of small manipulatives, such as buttons, plastic spiders, or beans, in different compartments of a box. Provide children with unsolved equations, word problems, or the Hands reproducible (page 68), and let them choose the manipulatives they want to use to solve the problems. Have children use the Hands reproducible as a math mat. Have them put an addition or subtraction sign in the center box. To make a record sheet, reduce the hands on the photocopier and fit three to five on a page. Have children draw in the equations they made on the math mat and record their answers.

Do-It-Yourself Dry Erase Boards

To make each child a dry erase board, purchase a large sheet of plain tile board from a hardware or home improvement store. Use a permanent marker and a yardstick to divide the board into equal-sized rectangles, one rectangle for each child. Have the board cut, or cut it yourself with a saw. Sand the edges of each small board, and you're ready to go! Tip: To preserve a child's work done on a board, photocopy it! If you're on a do-it-yourself roll, make two-sided, Velcro dry erase boards. Cut carpet squares to size, and glue one to the back of each dry-erase board. Give each child a board, an envelope with one fine-tip dry erase marker, a collection of laminated activity cards, and any manipulatives—with self-stick Velcro on the back—necessary to complete the activities.

D is for . . .

Dog Bones

Dog-bone treats come in a variety of sizes and colors, so they make perfect math manipulatives for activities such as adding, patterning, and graphing. Have children record the math work they did with the real dog-treat bones on the Dog-Bone Math reproducible (page 69). After children have used the dog-bone treats to complete the problems, have them color the paper bones to match the dog-bone treats, cut them out, and glue them to a sheet of paper in the order they have arranged the real ones.

Dominos

Gather several sets of dominos, and place them in a learning center. Include index cards with directions for activities such as the following:

- Single-Digit Math Problems—Invite children to place dominos vertically to make math problems. Have children record the number next to each square of dots, and write in the operation sign and answer. Have children use the Domino Math reproducible (page 70) for practice.
- Magic Squares—Have children find four dominos on which the two numbers on each domino will equal the same number when added or multiplied. For example, the domino with two dots on one side and three dots on the other equals five when added together. Children would look for three other dominos that also equal five when the sides are added. Have children place the dominos on a blank square of the Magic Squares reproducible (page 71) and draw each domino in the rectangles beside their work. Assign numbers for the center or invite children to choose their own.
- Fractions—On the Domino Fractions reproducible (page 72) have children draw the dominos that show each fraction.

A Word of Advice

DISCIPLINE

Make the work interesting and the discipline will take care of itself. —E. B. White

You can never eliminate all discipline problems in your classroom.
However, by making learning fun and interesting and by giving children choices,
you reduce discipline problems in your classroom.

E is for . . .

Easels

Use cardboard easels found at office supply stores to "advertise" activity directions, important messages, and activity menus (see page 36). Place self-stick Velcro on the easels and on the back of the information you want to display to use the same easels over and over.

Egg Cartons

Egg cartons make wonderful paperback bookstands. Turn an egg carton over, and make slits between each row of "bumps." Slip paperback books into the slits and you're done!

Eggs

Colorful plastic eggs are irresistible to children and are a terrific way to store manipulatives in a math center. Try using them with these ideas:

- Place a different kind of math manipulative, such as buttons, beans, or beads, in each egg. Place the eggs in a carton. Invite children to use the materials from one or more eggs to write and illustrate a math problem.
- Provide children with empty eggs and a bag of manipulatives, and invite them to sort the materials into separate eggs. Then, have children use the manipulatives to practice patterning.
- Fill the eggs with different colors of miniature jelly beans. Assign each color a different monetary value, and record the values on an index card. Glue the index card to the inside top of the egg carton. Invite children to pick one egg and graph the contents of the egg on the Jelly-Bean Graph reproducible (page 73). Then, have them use the jelly beans to solve the money problems on the Jelly-Bean Money reproducible (page 74). Invite children to eat their jelly beans when they are done and then replace the empty egg in the carton.

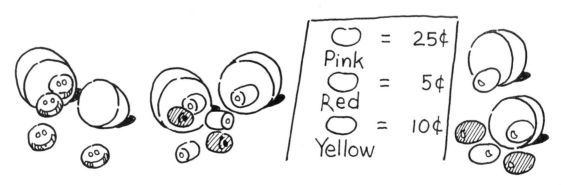

E is for . . .

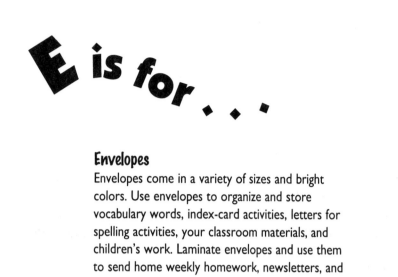

Envelopes

Envelopes come in a variety of sizes and bright colors. Use envelopes to organize and store vocabulary words, index-card activities, letters for spelling activities, your classroom materials, and children's work. Laminate envelopes and use them to send home weekly homework, newsletters, and notes to parents.

Erasers

For a unique learning center, turn over several felt-strip chalkboard erasers, and glue them together as shown. Invite children to slip letter cards, word cards, or picture cards between the slits to make words, alphabetize, or sequence a story. Write center directions on separate cards, and place them between the slits of a separate eraser.

A Word of Advice

ENVIRONMENT

When students enter kindergarten, they should discover that each class is a working, problem-solving unit and that each student has both individual and group responsibilities. —William Glasser

Build community in your classroom by giving children responsibilities for themselves and with others.
Not only is this good for children but it also makes your life easier.
Make it a rule not to do anything for children that they are able to do for themselves.

F is for . . .

Fabric

Use inexpensive fabric remnants in the following ways to make your classroom and lessons fun and exciting. (Look for seasonal, holiday, and thematic prints at a fabric store.)

● Use fabric to define the space for a learning center or work area. To do this, fold the fabric and place it in a container with all materials/manipulatives for the center or work area. Have children spread out the fabric on the floor and use the materials on the fabric only.

● For a great estimating, one-to-one correspondence, and place value activity, use the following directions: Obtain fabric printed with distinct objects placed far enough apart to allow a stacking cube to be placed over them. Divide the class into groups, and give each group a large piece of fabric and stacking cubes. Have groups estimate how many objects are on their piece. Then, ask groups to place one stacking cube on each object on their fabric until all objects are covered. Ask groups to take off the cubes and stack them in groups of ten. To close, have groups count the number of "tens" and "ones" they have to determine the number of objects on their fabric. Ask groups to compare that number to their estimation. (Modify this activity for children who are less advanced by asking them to place one stacking cube on each object for one-to-one correspondence.)

● Cut fabric to cover a cardboard box. Dip the fabric in diluted liquid starch, wring it out, cover the box with the wet fabric, and let it dry. Use the box to attractively display center directions or to store class materials.

● Have children make hardcover books and cover them with fabric instead of wallpaper.

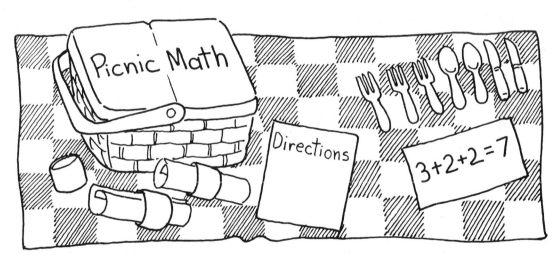

File Cabinet

Think about moving your file cabinet so it becomes a teaching tool. If you move the cabinet away from the wall, you instantly have two or three magnetic boards children can place magnetic letters on to create poetry, words, or sentences. In addition, you have a new place to hang children's work!

File Folders

File folders have so many uses! Try these ideas to get even more use from them:

● Plan your week with file folders. Label five file folders with the days of the week, and write *Next Week* on a sixth. As you write out your plans for each day, make a list of things you will need, and place it in the appropriate folder. As you come across papers you will need to photocopy, put them in the corresponding folder.

● Use file folders to create sticky-note record organizers. Write each child's name on an empty folder. Then, photocopy the Class List reproducible (page 75) twice, and write a child's name in each square. Glue the grids inside a new folder, laminate it, and place a pad of sticky notes in the folder. Write anecdotal or assessment information about each child on small sticky notes and place them on the corresponding space in the grid. When a sticky note is full, simply transfer it to the inside of the child's folder and begin writing on a new one.

● For a spelling center, cut thin strips of self-stick Velcro, and place the soft half of the Velcro horizontally, inside a file folder on the right side. Tape a resealable plastic bag on the top right corner of the open folder. Make a set of letter cards with squares of the rough half of the Velcro stuck to the back. Place the Velcro letter cards in the bag. Tape a spelling list on the top left corner of the open folder. Have children attach the letter cards to the Velcro strips to make their spelling words.

Flags and Banners

Have children use permanent markers or acrylic paint and a large piece of vinyl to design a flag to represent the class. Hang your flag or banner outside the door of your classroom each morning for children to see as they arrive.

Flashlights

Flashlights make great pointers for a Read the Room (see page 47) activity. Invite children to tour the room, read all the words and labels they see, and use the flashlight beam to highlight the words they are reading. Have students do this with the lights on or off.

F is for . . .

Flyswatters
Use flyswatters in the following ways to make learning lots of fun:
- Cut out the center of a flyswatter to make a fun "word framer" for children to use while reading the room.
- Make an overhead transparency that contains words you want children to find, such as compound words or words with contractions, short or long vowel sounds, or specific beginning sounds. Place it on an overhead projector. Fold a piece of white paper over a flyswatter, and tape it in place. Ask children to find the words that fit a chosen category. As children identify them, "swat" each word on the screen, then slowly move the flyswatter away from the screen. The word will *appear* to be pulled off the screen and onto the flyswatter. Return it to the screen by moving the flyswatter back to the screen. You will have children's undivided attention!

Fold and Crease
Fold and crease paper to save time and create useful materials like the following:
- Forget the ruler and use the "fold and crease" method to make straight grids for graphic organizers, graphs, and recording sheets. Decide how many boxes you want, and then make horizontal and vertical folds to create them. Cut off a row if you end up with one too many. Then, draw over the creases and reproduce!
- Fold and crease paper to make accordion books. Vary the size of the paper to make the books different lengths or widths. Tape sheets together to make longer books, or use adding machine tape or butcher paper.

A Word of Advice

FRIENDSHIP

The only way to have a friend is to be one. —Ralph Waldo Emerson

Your most valuable professional tools are your friends at school.
They are a support system and are there for sharing, caring, and brainstorming.
Be a friend and mentor to a new teacher. Be there for your teacher friends.
Everyone benefits in a school where the teachers are friends.

G is for . . .

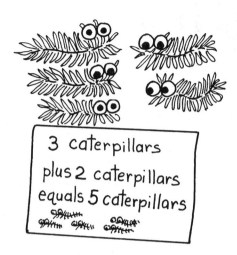

Garland

Cut apart plastic, metallic, and wood holiday garland to create fun and unique manipulatives for a math center or jewelry and costumes for a dramatic play center.

3 caterpillars
plus 2 caterpillars
equals 5 caterpillars

Gift Game

Each day or week, put inside a box something special, such as a prop that will introduce a theme or unit, a science material for an experiment, a math manipulative for a lesson, a new read-aloud poem, a new game, or a new piece of recess equipment. Gift wrap the box, and hide it. To introduce the gift game the first time, read aloud *Benjamin's 365 Birthdays* by Judi Barrett, a story about a dog that loves to open presents. Show children the box, pass it around, and invite each child to guess what's inside. Choose a child to open the box and display its contents. Ask children to guess why the object was placed in the box and how it will be used.

Glasses

Search garage sales and discount stores for eyeglasses or sunglasses with interesting frames. Pop out the lenses, and glue small objects, such as buttons, on the glasses to make them even more fun. Place several sets of glasses in a reading center. Invite children to wear the "magic glasses" when they read the room (i.e., tour the room and read aloud labels and words) or read to you and to designate that they are reading silently and don't wish to be disturbed.

Glasses For D.W. by Marc Brown

Chimps Don't Wear Glasses by Laura Numeroff

 **G is for . . .**

Glue

Glue is a necessity in every classroom, but keep the following things in mind:

- The first is to remember that glue should never be kept in children's desks. This is the black hole of education! The glue will only open, spill, and stick their new textbook pages together. Your children won't be able to find it when needed, and some will see it for the nutritional value only.
- Different kinds of glue should be used for different projects. White school glue is the old standby. Water it down, put it in lids, and have children use toothpicks or cotton swabs to apply it. Teach your children any expectations you have about how they use glue.
- Remove the tips of new glue bottles. Use a cotton swab to dab petroleum jelly on the inside of the tops to keep them from clogging.
- Glue sticks don't run . . . they just roll, but they may be a better idea for some projects.
- Rubber cement is my personal favorite. Use rubber cement to attach large butcher paper to the wall. When the paper is ready to come down it peels off. Anything left on the wall will "rub" off. Be sure to test this on a small space first.

Greeting Cards

Gather several greeting cards (at least one card for each child) with interesting images. Cover the words on the inside of each card with a piece of paper cut to size, and glue in place. Over several days, display each card, and invite children to brainstorm words they might use to write a story about each picture. Write the words on the inside of the card. Place the cards in a writing center for children to use for creative writing, or give each child a different card, and ask him or her to write a story about the picture. Use the cards again and again by giving children different cards each time.

G is for . . .

Guest Reader

Invite four or five children to each select a book to read to their classmates. Give them four days to practice reading, prepare questions to ask their audience, and select one prop. Establish an appropriate time limit (e.g., 15 minutes) for each child's reading and Q & A period. Have each reader post a sign-up sheet with his or her book title. Number each sheet so that the readers have audiences of equal sizes, and then have children sign up for the book they would like to hear.

The Old Man & His Door
1. Joe
2. Carrie
3. Marc
4. Antwan

Ice Bear and Little Fox
1. Akil
2. Crystal
3. Whitney
4. Jason

Dolphins
1. Chris
2. Daniel
3. Maurice
4. Angela

Hannah and the Seven Dresses
1. Felicia
2. Alycia
3. Devin
4. Jenny

A Word of Advice

GEOGRAPHY

Only those who will risk going too far can possibly find out how far one can go. —T. S. Eliot

Make geography a part of almost every lesson you teach!
Keep a globe, an atlas, and several maps handy, and use them when discussing
current events and locations described in stories and articles.
Bring geography into math lessons by talking about the locations of geometric structures,
such as the Pyramids or the Pentagon.

H is for . . .

Hallway
Think of the hallway as an extension of your classroom. If it's outside your door, use it! Invite children to take center work or group work into the hallway. And, of course, use hallway walls to display children's work!

Hats
Fill a hat rack or basket with hats, and place it in a writing center. Invite children to choose a hat, pretend to be a character who might wear it, and write a story about that character.

Hobby Hall
Ask each teacher to place a desk outside his or her classroom and create a display about a favorite hobby. When all the displays are up, have teachers take their children on a tour of "Hobby Hall" so they learn about hobbies, other teachers, and their school as a community. (This is a great activity for the beginning of the school year or for January, National Hobby Month.)

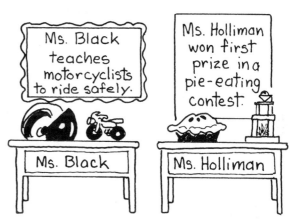

Horizontal Picture Holders
Obtain several horizontal picture holders and three-ring binders at an office supply store. Place in the holders 4" x 6" (10 cm x 15 cm) index cards with activity directions; class photos; magnetic letters, words, or pictures; stickers; or paper or felt cutouts. Insert the holders into labeled three-ring binders for easy reference.

Hula Hoops
Use hula hoops to define personal work space for "floor work." Use hula hoops during center time to define space and give children boundaries. If your classroom is carpeted, place self-stick Velcro on one side of each hoop to hold it in place.

A Word of Advice
HUMOR

A very wise old teacher once said: "I consider a day's teaching is wasted if we do not all have one hearty laugh."
He meant that when people laugh together, they cease to be young and old, master and pupils, workers and driver, jailer and prisoners, they become a single group of human beings enjoying its existence. —Gilbert Albert

Humor is so important! Work on finding humor in the classroom—
laugh more with the children, your colleagues, and your family at home. It's good for you!

I is for . . .

Ice Cube Trays

Ice cube trays make wonderful mini-organizers. They are perfect containers for small math manipulatives, magnetic letters, small word cards, and more. Use the trays for sorting activities, too. When children work on a specific math skill, have them use a variety of materials organized in the ice cube trays. The trays conveniently stack for compact storage when not in use.

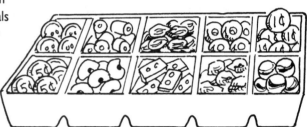

Ideas

A great way to spark ideas for using inexpensive materials in new, creative ways is to go to craft, office supply, hardware, or discount stores and go up and down the aisles looking at stuff. Think about each item's possibilities, not how it is "supposed" to be used. A bag of flower petals on a markdown shelf becomes math manipulatives, a rolodex becomes a way to organize menu activities, fabric remnants become boundaries for mobile centers, and so on.

Instant Programs

Instant programs—class skits, plays, and musical performances—are derived from many books. Any book with a combination of information, music or poetry, and interesting characters or situations can form the basis for a wonderful class program. Write lyrics or poetry stanzas on overhead transparencies for easy reference, sing-alongs, or read-alongs. Have children make props and costumes. Help children think of appropriate narration, and put a great class program together in an instant! Use the following book suggestions to get started:

> *Do Cowboys Ride Bikes?* by Kathy Tucker
> *Do Pirates Take Baths?* by Kathy Tucker
> *Yankee Doodle* by Gary Chalk

is for . . .

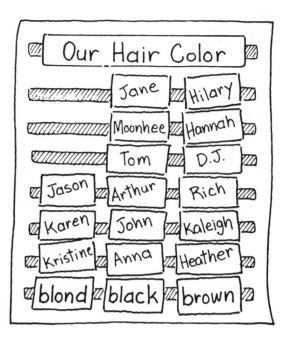

Interactive Charts

Make your own interactive charts. Choose the graphic organizers and charts you use the most, and use permanent markers to draw them on vinyl. Apply self-stick Velcro in horizontal or vertical strips onto the vinyl. Place the other half of the self-stick Velcro strips on letter, word, or picture cards; cut apart book pages; or anything else (e.g., words, phrases, and pictures) you want children to sort, graph, or organize.

Interesting Information

Choose a specific time each week for children to share interesting information about a current topic of study, a current event, or anything new they have "discovered." Invite children to display illustrations, news clippings, or visual recordings of the information on a bulletin board. Or, compile recordings of each week's information in a class book.

A Word of Advice

IMAGINATION

Imagination is more important than knowledge. —Albert Einstein

Imagination is one of the best things you have to create meaningful activities.
Look around at the things you have, and imagine how they *can* be used rather than how they are supposed to be used.
Look at your curriculum, and imagine how you can make learning both interesting and fun with more interactive, hands-on, and thought-provoking activities.

 is for . . .

Jars

Collect clear, plastic jars of several shapes and sizes, and try these helpful uses for them:

- Keep a variety of different-sized math manipulatives in the jars for partner and group work. Have children examine the jars and estimate how many things are inside. Then, have children empty the jars and refill them to count, sort, and make patterns.
- Use jars to store your markers, pushpins, colored pencils, and other supplies. Keep your materials in plain view to avoid having to hunt and search for them.

Jewelry

Search garage sales and discount stores for costume jewelry to be used in the following ways:
- Place the jewelry in your dramatic play center or class store.
- Detach beads and "jewels" to use as math manipulatives.
- Use whole pieces of jewelry or individual parts for arts and crafts projects.

Jigsaw Puzzle Pieces

What can you do with puzzles with missing pieces? Use these ideas to give new life to them:
- Use them as math manipulatives. Spray-paint the decorated side of each piece. Have children use the pieces to show addition, subtraction, multiplication, and division problems.
- Give each child a different puzzle piece. Have children glue their piece, decorated side up, to construction paper and draw around it to create a scene from the decorated piece.
- Have children glue craft supplies (e.g., feathers, felt, colored packing "peanuts") and several puzzle pieces on paper to make a collage.

One puzzle piece plus one puzzle piece equals two puzzle pieces.
Nan

J is for . . .

Journals

Take journals a step further by providing whole-class journals as well as individual journals. Place the journals in appropriate places around the classroom, such as next to the cage of a new class pet, on the counter beside the seed-growing experiments, and even near the window. Invite children to record observations, questions, and comments in the journals as they visit each place. Read the journals at least once a week to respond to children's thoughts and ideas.

> I like the way the butterfly's tongue uncurls.
> – Pam
>
> Pam,
> Did you know butterflies smell with their antennae and taste with their feet?
> Ms. Jones

Jump Ropes

Jump-rope rhymes are poetry in motion! Teach the class some jump-rope rhymes, and take children outside to recite them as they jump individually and in groups. Then, if from your classroom you are able to see your children outside, place jump ropes and rhymes near the door for children to use as an outdoor poetry center. Children jump and chant as they enjoy language arts! Sources for jump-rope poetry include the following:

> *Anna Banana: 101 Jump Rope Rhymes* by Joanna Cole
> *The Jump Rope Book* by Elizabeth Loredo
> *Red Hot Peppers: The Skookum Book of Jump Rope Games, Rhymes, and Fancy Footwork*
> by Diane and Bob Boardman

A Word of Advice

JUDGMENT

Everyone complains of his memory, and no one complains of his judgment. —La Rochefoucauld

As classroom teachers we make judgments every day
about what we do, how we do it, and the children with whom we work.
We always work to make good judgments as professionals.
Review, reflect, and don't be afraid to reconsider if necessary!

K is for . . .

Kabob Cooking
For a fun math activity, cut pieces of fruit, cheese, and lunch meat into small pieces. Have children create different patterns with the food as they carefully place the pieces on toothpicks or long sandwich picks.

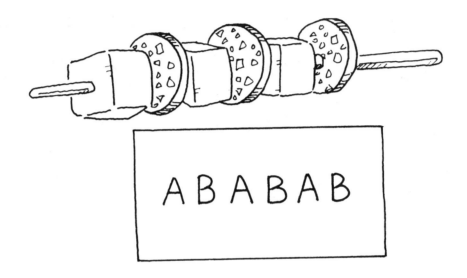

Ketchup Week
On those short weeks before vacation, display a bottle of ketchup and proclaim the week to be Ketchup Week! Change the weekly routine to include time for review, classroom reorganization, and designated "ketchup sessions" during which children are encouraged to "catch up" on assignments.

Key Chains
Obtain several interesting key chains from grand openings, giveaways, and even your "junk drawer" at home. Laminate index cards with vocabulary words for reading, math, science, a seasonal or thematic unit, or any other subject. Hole-punch the top left corner of each card. Place related groups of cards on each key chain, and display the cards on a bulletin board titled *Words to Know*. Invite pairs of children to take a group of cards and quiz their partner on spelling, definitions, or word usage.

K is for . . .

Key Rack

Hang a key rack near your classroom door. Use the rack to hang items such as a whistle, a "pen necklace," cabinet keys, or anything else you use frequently.

Kool-Aid® Packages

Ask parents to send in empty Kool-Aid packages. Laminate each package, and invite children to use them for sorting, matching, or placing flavor names in alphabetical order.

A Word of Advice

KNOWING

If you have knowledge, let others light their candles by it. —Margaret Fuller

Our job is to encourage and set the stage for children to want to know.
One of the ways we do that is to want to know ourselves.
Share with children your curiosity; model the love of "knowing."
This also applies to teachers as professionals.
We never know enough and are always wanting to know more.

 **L is for . . .**

Lazy Susans

Put containers of markers, scissors, colored pencils, tape, glue, and any other materials children use on a lazy Susan in the middle of the "teacher table." Invite children to slowly spin the lazy Susan to get the materials they need.

Letter Sorts

Use this learning-center activity to help children learn to identify both capital and lowercase letters regardless of their font styles. Use your word processing program to make $1^{3}/_{4}$" (4.5 cm) squares and place a letter in each square. Use a variety of fonts for the letters. Print the page, laminate it, and cut apart the letter cards for children to sort.

Letter Writing

Letter writing is an important life skill, so help your children write and send different kinds of letters throughout the year. Try the following ideas to make letter writing fun and interesting:

● Read aloud *Messages in the Mailbox* by Loreen Leedy. Then, invite children to write friendly letters to friends and family members.
● Ask children to name some toys with which they are very satisfied or very disappointed. Show children how to write business letters to express their thoughts and suggestions for improvement.
● As a class, choose a proposition that is being considered in your town or county. Help children write persuasive "letters to the editor" to convince voters to vote for or against the idea.
● Have children write to the authors and illustrators of their favorite books.

L is for . . .

Lima Beans

Lima beans aren't just for sneaking to the dog anymore! Try these creative ways of getting them out of your cupboard:

- Buy a bag of large, dry lima beans. Use a thin-tipped permanent marker to write one letter of the alphabet on each bean. Make two sets, one uppercase and one lowercase, for each letter. Invite children to use the beans for spelling practice, crossword puzzles, matching games, and any other letter or word activity.
- Use lima beans as markers for games such as multiplication bingo.

Luggage

Obtain sets of old, small luggage from garage sales or parent donations. Then, try these two uses for them:

- Store in the luggage entire learning centers, including manipulatives, art supplies, and even books. Label the outside of each luggage piece so children know what's inside.
- Put a favorite book, a stuffed animal, and a journal in a suitcase. Give children a turn to take home the suitcase and write in the journal about the adventures the stuffed animal had with them out of school.

L is for . . .

Lumberyards

Lumberyards are a great source for building materials for your classrooms. You can often convince owners to donate wood scraps (large and small) or provide them at minimal cost. Use the wood scraps for art activities, measurement, counting, geometry, and more!

Lunch

At the beginning of the year, invite several children to have lunch with you once a week in the classroom. Make the lunch special by using place mats, a flower centerpiece, and real silverware. Take the time to talk and ask questions informally so everyone has a chance to get to know each other.

A Word of Advice

NO LOOSEY GOOSEY

Not to know is bad; not to wish to know is worse. —African Proverb

Avoid being "loosey goosey" about what goes on in your classroom.
Always have a master plan with clear goals for your children.
Be sure you know exactly how you are going to reach those goals.

M is for . . .

Magic Spray

Use this idea when children come in after a long, hot recess and you will be reading aloud to them. As children enter the room, spray a can of "magic spray" (air freshener) as an invitation for children to join you in your read-aloud area. Use the same scented spray every time you read aloud throughout the year. Children will love it and have a pleasant memory to connect with their reading experiences.

Magic Tree

String white or colored Christmas lights on a silk fig tree (like the ones in restaurants) to create a "magic tree." Each day plug in the tree lights during your opening activities. Then, invite children to stand under the magic tree when they need to read the really hard words. It's magic! It works!

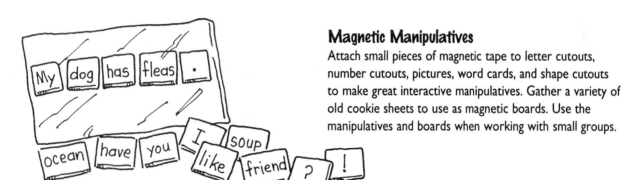

Magnetic Manipulatives

Attach small pieces of magnetic tape to letter cutouts, number cutouts, pictures, word cards, and shape cutouts to make great interactive manipulatives. Gather a variety of old cookie sheets to use as magnetic boards. Use the manipulatives and boards when working with small groups.

Marshmallow Number Stands

Give each child a marshmallow. Have children place their marshmallow on their desk, flat side down, and carefully push a sandwich pick (longer than a toothpick) through the center of the marshmallow to make a "number stand." Give each child several pieces of "O" cereal, such as Cheerios®. Say a number, and ask children to stack that number of cereal pieces on their number stand. After children check their answer with a partner, invite them to eat the cereal and play again. Have older children make three number stands to represent ones, tens, and hundreds. Say a three-digit number aloud, and have children stack the cereal on the stands to show the number.

M is for . . .

Master Planning

Where are you going? What are you doing? When are you going to do it? Use a large piece of paper, at least ledger size, or the inside of a legal-size file folder to make a chart that has a row for each month you teach, a column for each curriculum area, and a column for *Other*. Label each box by month, and then write in the themes that are non-negotiable like holidays. Then, take a look at your curriculum. What are your big math, science, and social studies units? What field trips are you planning? When is state testing? Write those in. This helps you see the big picture, where you are going, how you are going to get there, and how everything is linked together.

Menus

Use paper, markers, and a laminating machine to make "activity menus" that give children choices for self-directed activities. Create a menu for each subject area, place appropriate materials with each menu, and invite children to get started!

Metal Pails

Place magnetic manipulatives (see page 35) in large metal pails to make mobile learning centers. Include task cards to give children an opportunity for self-directed learning. Have children arrange the manipulatives on the outside of the pails to spell, match word pairs, make equations, and more!

A Word of Advice
MIND AND MEMORY

Education means developing the mind, not stuffing the memory. —Anonymous

Help children become problem solvers and critical thinkers.
This combination makes for lifetime learners. Is some "memory stuffing" necessary?
Yes, but developing a curious mind, a love of learning, and a thirst for knowledge is always better.
Include both rote learning and problem solving in your curriculum,
and if you must err, err on the side of developing the mind.

Name Necklaces

At the beginning of the year, give each child a 2' (61 cm) piece of yarn and a stack of index-card halves—half an index card for each child in the class. Ask children to write each classmate's name on an index card, hole-punch a corner of each card, and string the cards onto the yarn to make a "name necklace." Invite children to wear their necklace during the first week of school to show their class pride.

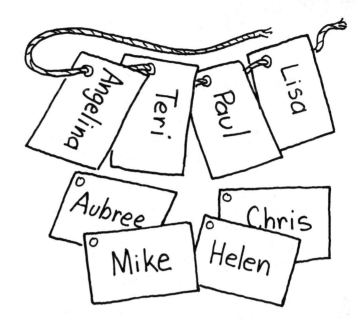

Napkin Rings

Obtain several sets of seasonal napkin rings at garage sales or discount stores. Roll up center or activity directions, and place each set of directions in a different napkin ring. Place the rings in the appropriate center or classroom location for a fun way to organize activity directions!

Nests

Find abandoned bird's nests in the winter, and save them to use for this springtime science activity. Place a bird's nest in a shallow bowl, and water it like a plant. Keep the nest in a sunny spot. The nest will absorb the water, and the seeds deposited by the birds will sprout and grow. Keep the nest watered as needed. Children are amazed by this experiment. Put a class journal next to the bowl, and encourage children to write their predictions and observations.

Newspapers

Use newspapers in your classroom for all curriculum areas. Have children go on a "word search," hunting for short and long vowel words, nouns, verbs, adjectives, prefixes, and suffixes. Place newspapers in a writing center so children can cut out words to create a story. Use grocery ads in a math center for addition, subtraction, and problem-solving activities.

N is for . . .

Noodles

Keep handy bags of dry noodles in a variety of shapes for the following activities:

- Invite children to glue noodles to paper to create words, demonstrate math equations, or create "special effects" in art projects.
- Invite children to use noodles to make a sculpture.
- Mix food coloring in alcohol, and color noodles. After they have dried, invite children to use them with yarn or string to make a necklace with a pattern.

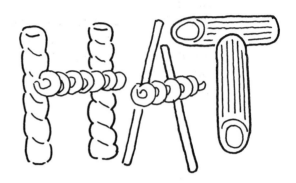

Note Necklaces

Create a convenient place to keep notes and records of child observations. Cut a file folder into a rectangle on the fold so that it will open into a 10" x 5" (25 cm x 12.5 cm) rectangle. Cut several pieces of paper into 9" x 4" (23 cm x 10 cm) rectangles. Fold the paper in half, place it inside the folder, and hold it in place with a rubber band along the "spine." Punch two holes on the right side of the folded file folder to create a place to slip in a pencil. Punch a hole in the top left corner of the folded paper, add a piece of yarn, and tie the yarn in a loop to make a necklace. Wear the necklace whenever you are observing children working independently. Add new paper each time the book is filled.

Nuts

Nuts, both edible and hardware store nuts, make perfect manipulatives for math. Have children use them for counting, fact families, measurement, and estimation.

A Word of Advice

NOTES TO PARENTS

The greatest good you can do for another is not just to share your riches, but to reveal to him his own. —Benjamin Disraeli

Communicating with parents is one of the most important tasks you have as an educator. Keep it simple, with frequent brief notes that let parents know what takes place in your classroom and include some positive news for parents about their own children.

O is for...

Odds and Ends

Odds and ends belong in the "treasure box" for art, exploration, problem solving, and more. Send home a note at the beginning of the year, inviting parents to send in items such as cardboard tubes (for art projects and creative play), Pringles® cans (see page 43 for ideas), paper plates (for arts and crafts as well as for food), laundry detergent caps (for puppet and doll "hats" and paint/water containers), and film canisters (for individual paste holders). Send home additional notes throughout the year as needs arise.

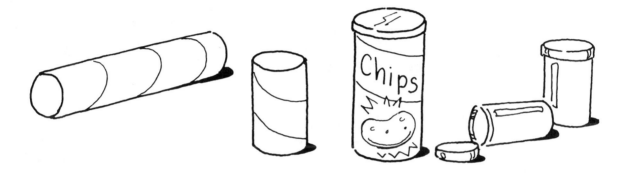

Outrageous Outfits

There should be a bit of "Ms. Frizzle" in all of us! Whenever you begin a new unit or theme, or just before a holiday or special celebration, go through your closet, and put together an outrageous outfit related to the topic to make a real impact on children. Try a combination of themed neckties, scarves, vests, glasses, shoes, and hats. To make an interchangeable outfit, cut shapes from self-stick felt, and glue them to a denim skirt. Your children will remember skills and concepts when they are presented by a teacher who dresses for the occasion!

Overalls

Use some old denim overalls in lots of ways. Here are just a few:

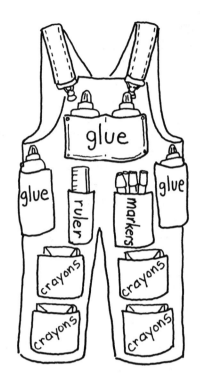

- Overalls make a great organizer! Sew on additional colorful pockets to store scissors, markers, rulers, and other important tools.
- Pin ant-shaped name cards to overall pockets to make a cute helper chart. Use a permanent marker to write *We Have Worker Ants in Our Pants!* as a heading on the overalls. Velcro to each pocket a card with the job that "ant" is responsible for.
- Stuff overalls with books, activity directions, crayons, or any other supply to make a fun, portable learning center.

Overhead Projectors

Overhead projectors aren't just by the podium anymore. Try these two ideas:

- Make a transparency of a background, such as a forest, and project it for children to use it as a background and spotlight for a puppet show or role playing.
- Use a spare overhead projector for a great learning center. Turn activity sheets from your current curriculum into transparencies for children to use with overhead markers. Be creative when making the transparencies—use rubber stamps, computer clip art, or handmade drawings.

A Word of Advice

OLD

Experience teaches. —Tacitus

Old is not always a bad thing. "Old" teachers have much to offer in the way of experience, support, and empathy.
"Old" activities are many times tried and true—and they work!
Remember, "Something old, something new, something borrowed, something glued!"

P is for . . .

Paper-Cup Stacks and Lines

Have children stack or line up paper cups in the following ways for some hands-on learning fun!

- Write a different number (counting by ones, twos, fives, or any number pattern) on individual cups. Have children stack or line up cups in numerical order.
- Write a different letter on each of 26 cups. Have children stack or line up the cups in alphabetical order.
- Write each letter from a spelling word on individual cups. Have children stack or line up the cups to spell the word.
- Write each word from a sentence on individual cups. Ask children to stack or line up the cups to "rebuild" the sentence.
- Set up ten cups in four rows like bowling pins for this rainy-day activity. Invite children to use a foam or tennis ball to "bowl over" the cups. Have children use their "bowling score" to create a subtraction problem. For example, a child who knocks over seven cups might write 10 – 7 = 3.

Paper-Plate Book Covers

To begin, get together with several other teachers to have a paper-plate swap. Have each person bring in a package of decorated paper plates. Invite each teacher to choose different paper plates that work well with his or her units, writing-process lessons, or themes, and take the number of plates he or she brought to the swap. Invite children to write stories on inexpensive blank paper plates. Then, bind their "pages" together between two decorated paper plates. Have children write a title and their name on the first page.

Pencil Boxes

Keep children from sharpening pencils at an inappropriate time with this neat trick. Label and display two plastic boxes, one with the word *sharp* and one with the word *dull*. Instead of passing out pencils at the beginning of the year, sharpen two for each child, and place them in the "sharp" box. Have children pick up a sharp pencil in the morning, and as pencils break or become dull, have them place their pencil in the "dull" box and retrieve a new one from the sharp box. At the end of the day, have a child helper sharpen all the dull pencils and place them in the sharp box for the next day.

P is for . . .

Picnic-Basket Center

Check garage sales, discount stores, and flea markets for old picnic baskets. Place inside a basket a tablecloth for a work mat as well as plastic foods, plates, and utensils. Create an index-card label for each item in the basket. Invite children to have a pretend picnic and set their places with table settings and food. Have them place each word card next to each object. Add a journal to the basket for more fluent writers to describe their ideal picnic. Picnic baskets can also hold books, manipulatives, and much more. Any activity is a "picnic" using this unique container.

tablecloth

plate

cheese

milk

fork

Pillowcase Book Record

Place in your reading center several pillows covered with white pillowcases. Each time a child reads a book, have him or her use fabric markers to record on a pillowcase the name of the book, the author, and a book rating from one to ten (ten being the best). Change pillowcases when they are full of recordings, and hang them like banners in the reading center.

Place Mats

Look for vinyl place mats at discount stores, at garage sales, or in your own kitchen. Keep an eye out for place mats that are seasonal, holiday oriented, or thematic, such as geography, dinosaur, or number place mats. Trim sharp corners, and bind sheets of blank paper—ledger size fits perfectly when folded in half—between each pair to make blank class books. Throughout the year, as appropriate situations arise, have children create class books using the place-mat books. Have children write their title on the first inside page.

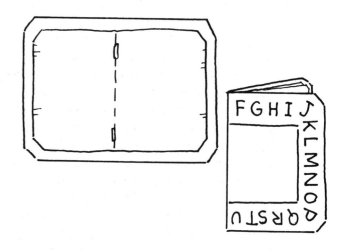

P is for . . .

Pocket Chart

Make your own pocket chart by stapling the reinforced sides of clear page protectors horizontally to a bulletin board. Slide sentence strips, photographs, index cards, or other materials into the protectors.

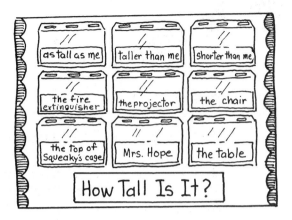

Poetry

Make poetry a daily part of your schedule and curriculum. Use poetry to introduce and review skills and concepts. Always start with rhyming words regardless of children's age, next teach couplets, and then each month teach children how to write a different kind of poem. Also use poetry for handwriting activities.

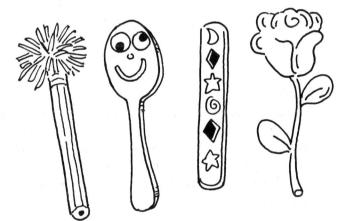

Pointers

Pointers for Read the Room (see page 47) should be fun! Don't start with the traditional pointer—the long stick with the apple on it. That is a lethal weapon in the hands of a child. Start short and model appropriate pointer behavior. Try using pencils with toppers first, and then progress to wooden spoons with wiggly eyes, star wands, silk flowers, and spatulas. Hot-glue small stuffed animals on dowels to create theme pointers.

Pringles®-Can Tales

Record the first paragraph of a class story on a blank piece of construction paper. Place the paper in a Pringles can with a blank piece of paper and a small roll of tape. Place the can on a child's desk the next day, and invite him or her to write on the blank paper a paragraph that adds on to the story the class started the day before. Ask the child to illustrate his or her addition and tape it to the first page. Have the child roll up the papers, place them with a new blank sheet in the can, and pass it to a classmate. Continue the activity until everyone adds on to the story. Read aloud the story every few days to see how it is progressing. When everyone has a turn, have the class think of an ending to add to the last child's page. Store the completed story in the reading center.

P is for . . .

Print Shops

Here's a way to solve your paper problems. Visit your local print or copy shop and ask for scrap paper. They will usually fill a box with paper of a variety of colors and sizes. Use the paper in centers, class books, and art projects. In your classroom newsletter or a note home to parents, be sure to mention the name of the shop so parents with printing needs can repay the shop for its generosity by becoming customers.

Project Boards

Tri-fold project boards make wonderful learning-center displays. Cut the boards in half lengthwise, and then write in the middle of a board the name of the center. Attach Velcro tape to the side boards, the backs of directions, menus, and examples to create interchangeable parts.

A Word of Advice

PRESENTATION

A kind heart is a fountain of gladness, making everything in its vicinity into smiles. —Washington Irving

A lovely presentation makes a difference in your classroom! Take a look around your room from a child's point of view.
Is it warm and inviting? Does it reflect what children learn and are involved in?
Presentation of materials, activities, books, and more makes a huge difference
in how children respond to all kinds of curriculum.

Q is for . . .

Question Quilts

Question Quilts are versatile and are a great way to organize and display menus and directions. Make your own out of resealable plastic bags. Cut card stock slightly smaller than the bags, and write directions for a variety of theme-related activities on each card. Slide each card into a bag. Hole-punch the corners of each bag, avoiding the paper, and use yarn, pipe cleaners, or twist ties to tie the corners of the bags together. To create a new Question Quilt, replace the cards with a new set of theme- or curriculum-related cards, storing the previous set for use next year.

Questions and Answers

How many times have you asked, *Do you have a question?* and the reply is *My dog ran away last night?* The concept of questions and answers is a hard one for young children to understand. Use *How Many Bugs In a Box* by David Carter to introduce asking and telling sentences. Then try these ideas:

- Make a large question mark and period out of butcher paper, and write simple sentences on strips of paper, leaving off the punctuation. Read aloud the sentences, and have children sort them into questions and statements. Invite volunteers to use putty or masking tape to stick the sentences onto the large butcher-paper punctuation marks. Transfer this activity to a learning center for children to continue their practice.
- Draw a large question mark in the center of a 12" x 18" (30.5 cm x 46 cm) sheet of paper. Display the paper on Monday, and challenge each child to write one question in black on the paper. Invite children to read the questions and write their answers in red.

45

Q is for . . .

Quill Pens
Quills are an exciting addition to a writing center. Purchase large red, white, and blue feathers at a craft store, and cut a diagonal point on the tip of each one. Have children use poster paint (for "ink") to write on white paper in the manner of our forefathers.

Quotation Marks
Children find quotation marks hard to understand, so use the Frog and Toad books by Arnold Lobel to introduce or review them. Then, have children write dialogue and glue elbow macaroni to their paper to indicate quotation marks. They love this kinesthetic activity.

A Word of Advice

QUICK, QUICK, HURRY, HURRY (NO!)

Ordinary people merely think how they shall spend their time, a man of talent tries to use it. —Arthur Schopenhauer

We are always rushing ourselves and our children. Evaluate how you are spending your time.
Don't think of your day as chopped-up blocks of time. All teachers have the same amount of time . . . it's called our day.
Children pick up where they left off when they come back to the classroom.

R is for . . .

Raffle

Each time a child turns in homework on time, give him or her a raffle ticket. Have children write their name on the back of the ticket and drop it in a container. On a regular basis, draw out a ticket and award that child a special treat.

Read the Room

Read the Room is a simple and effective activity for your classroom. Because you already have a print-rich environment this activity takes virtually no extra effort from you. Have two or three children at a time (no more) quietly point to each word and read the print around the room.

Restaurant Supply Store

Restaurant supply stores are a great place to hunt for and gather containers, signs, and sign holders for your classroom. These materials are sturdy and hold up under repeated use.

Rocks

Rocks make wonderful manipulatives for center activities like the following:

● Pick up small, smooth rocks on the beach or purchase them at an aquarium supply store. Use a permanent marker to write a letter, word, or number on each rock. Have children use the rocks to make words; build sentences; make number sentences; or sort by size, shape, or weight.

● Have each child select a rock and write a description of it on an index card. Have children write their name on the bottom of a small paper bag and place their rock inside the bag. Collect the index cards. When each child has written a card, give each child a description. Challenge children to look through the bags to find the rock that matches their description. When this activity is done, conclude with a class discussion on effective description in writing.

R is for . . .

Round-Robin Sharing

Round-Robin Sharing provides every child in the class with an opportunity to share in less than five minutes. Divide the class into two groups. Have the first group sit in a small circle facing out. Have the second group sit in a large circle around the small circle facing in so that the two circles of children face each other. Set a timer for two minutes and have the inside circle share. Then, set the timer for an additional two minutes and have the outside circle share. You may want to ask a few of children to share with the whole class based on what you heard and observed.

Rubber Bands

Rubber bands have many uses in the classroom. After setting clear expectations for their use with your children, try these activities:

- Use the following directions to make a "poof book" with a rubber-band binding.
  1. Fold a sheet of paper in half widthwise. Fold it again in the same direction.
  2. Fold the paper in half in the opposite direction.
  3. Open the paper to a half sheet. Starting from the folded edge, cut along the crease. Stop where the fold lines intersect.
  4. Completely open the paper.
  5. Fold the paper lengthwise.
  6. Grasp the outer edges, and push them towards the center. The opening should "poof" out. Keep pushing until a book of four sections is formed.
  7. Fold the pages closed.
  8. Repeat steps 1–7 with a second piece of paper.
  9. Wrap a rubber band around the center of both poof books to create one book. This will create a 15-page book plus one page for the cover.

- Hole-punch the top and bottom of a simple half-fold book. Choose a straight object that is the same length as the book (e.g., pencil, plastic spoon, stick), and place it over the holes. Push one end of a rubber band up through the top hole and the other end through the bottom hole, and pull both loops around the ends of the straight object. Your book is bound together in a unique way. Use sticks for nature books, spoons or forks for nutrition books, or chopsticks for an information book about China.

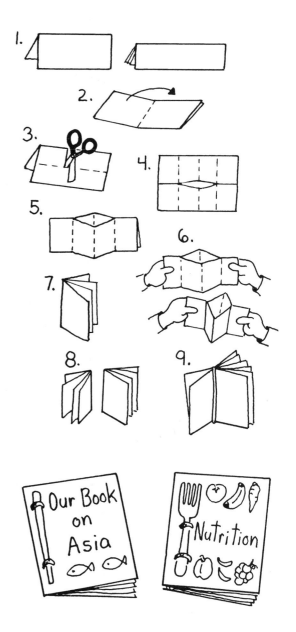

R is for . . .

Rulers

Rulers make a terrific binding for class books. Find two plastic rulers with holes. Have each child create a page for the class book. Punch holes along the side of the pages that line up with the holes in the rulers. Place the rulers back to back with the papers in between, and thread yarn, ribbon, or twine through the holes to hold the book together. This is a great binding for a book on class rules, measurement, or *If I ruled the world . . . .*

Rules

Make children a part of creating classroom rules by celebrating National Smile Week the first week of school. Make two large smiling lips out of butcher paper. On the first write *Things That Make Children Smile,* and on the second write *Things That Make the Teacher Smile.* Have children tell you what you could do in the classroom to make them smile. Record their suggestions on the children butcher-paper lips. Now ask what children do in the classroom to make you smile. Record their suggestions on the teacher lips. You and your children have created the class rules!

A Word of Advice

REVISIT AND REVIEW

Education should include knowledge of what to do with it. —Anonymous

Revisit and review should be an important part of your curriculum.
As you look at your year and your curriculum, plan to revisit and review skills and concepts on a regular basis.
Learning centers are a great place to do this.

S is for . . .

Seating Charts

Draw a blank seating chart on an 8½" x 11" (21.5 cm x 28 cm) sheet of paper. Cut small sticky notes into thirds, and write each child's name on a strip. Place the strips on their corresponding "desk" in your seating chart. When you move children, simply move the sticky notes to keep the chart up to date. Place the finished chart in a gallon-size resealable plastic bag, and hang it in an accessible spot.

Seed Packets

Seed packets are cheap at the end of the planting season, so scoop them up! Young children can use them for sorting, matching, and playing concentration. Older children can put them in alphabetical order, answer comprehension questions using the information on the back, or use a Venn diagram to compare and contrast the information on two packets.

Sewing Cards

Turn foam plates into simple "sewing cards." Draw a shape, letter, or number on each plate, and have children use plastic tapestry needles to punch through the plate and sew around their art. Tie one end of the yarn to the needles so you do not have to repeatedly rethread them.

Shaving Cream

Shaving cream is cheap and smells good! Use shaving cream to clean desks for Open House, as a motivator at a spelling center, and as part of a quick and fun way to renew and review skills. Add a plastic tray and shaving cream to the spelling center so children can practice their words by tracing the letters in the foam.

S is for . . .

Shoe Boxes and Bags

Shoe boxes and bags are a wonderful organizational tool. Use them to hold markers, scissors, hole punches, and other teaching tools. You may even want to have two, one at each end of the room, for children to return materials. Shoe boxes and bags also make great mailboxes for children.

Silverware

Plastic silverware in a variety of colors is a creative addition to your math center. Have children use it for counting, sorting, and patterning. Trace around the silverware to create recording sheets, and have children use crayons or markers to recreate the colorful patterns they made.

Smiles

This fun measuring activity requires measuring tape and a good case of the giggles. Give each pair of children a measuring tape, a blank piece of paper, and a clipboard. Invite them to write their names and measure each other's smiles and then circulate throughout the class, gathering more "smile data." Have children write the name of each person they measure and the length of his or her smile. When each pair has discovered the length of 15 smiles, have children return to their seats and graph their results.

Stamping Kits

Rubber stamps are a must for math, writing, and ABC centers. Teach your children to store stamp pads facedown so the ink will go to the top of the pad. Try these ideas for using rubber stamps:

- Have children stamp out fact families and patterns and use them to illustrate story problems at a math center.
- Have children create their own rebus stories in a writing center and use stamps in an ABC center to practice alphabetical order.
- Provide each child with one rubber stamp. Have children estimate how many of their design they can stamp on a piece of paper. Have them write that number on one side of the paper. Then, invite children to fill the other side of the page with that stamp to discover the answer. When children are done, have them return to the first side of the paper and write a sentence that compares their estimate with the exact amount.

S is for...

Stringing Blocks

Blocks with holes in them make a great activity for a spelling or "wonderful word center." Use a permanent marker to write a letter on each side of the blocks. Have children use yarn to string together the blocks to create words. For older children, you could write words for them to string into simple sentences or place in alphabetical order.

Stuffed Animals

Stuffed animals in a reading center give your emergent or reluctant readers someone to read to and keep them company while they take new risks in reading.

Swimming Pools

A blow-up pool or small plastic pool is a great addition to your reading center! Use it to define space and make your reading center a popular spot. Add pillows and this center makes a "splash" with children!

A Word of Advice

STUDENTS AND STYLES

All students can learn. —Christopher Morley

Every child in your classroom can learn. You know your curriculum, now look at your children. Identify their learning styles, or simply think of them in terms of auditory, visual, and kinesthetic learners. Make sure that as you are planning your introduction of skills and concepts that you include examples, activities, and demonstrations that meet the needs of the different learning styles in your classroom.

T is for...

Tables

You have to earn furniture in education! It sometimes takes several years to accumulate an extra table in your classroom, so here are some ways to use tables wisely when you get them:

● Use masking tape or colorful cloth tape to create areas and define new spaces. Tape down the middle in both directions and you have created four work spaces. Be creative. Manage materials and maintain organization by taping a box to show where the markers go and an X to show where to return the scissors.

● An easy way to create a puppet stage or a background for children to act out stories is through a "Table Tilt." Cover a table with a piece of white paper, and have children draw or paint a background or scenery. Tilt the table over on its side, and you are ready for a "production"!

Tackle Boxes

Tackle boxes are a great way to create a mobile materials kit. Store markers, glue, scissors, and other "teaching tools" in the tackle box so you can quickly move from one spot to the next and not have to go "fishing" for them.

Tall Tales

Tall tales give children an opportunity to use their imagination to "remember big" (i.e., remember something that really happened, but make it better and bigger) and stretch the truth when writing. Give each child a long strip of adding machine tape. Ask children to fold their tape into thirds, fourths, or more and then turn it so that each frame is a long thin rectangle. Encourage children to use each frame to tell how their story progresses. Have children use half of each frame to illustrate their sentences.

T is for . . .

Tape Recorders

Keep a tape recorder close at hand so that when you read aloud to your class you can tape as you read. Keep the tape running after the story to record the discussion with your children. When they listen to the tape, children love to hear the discussion and listen for their own voice. Keep the tapes at a listening center with copies of the book. Also, have children tape books they have practiced reading aloud. Encourage children to read with fluency and expression, and then add these "child made" tapes to a listening center.

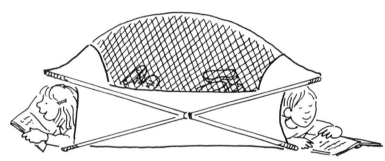

Tents

Tents for two are a tremendous addition to your classroom. Use them for a center or reading area. Place appropriate materials inside the tent, and invite children to crawl into their workplace. Leave the rain covers off so you can monitor children through the mosquito netting.

Themes

Organize materials, curriculum, and your school year through the use of themes. Let your science and social studies curriculum guide your choice of themes, and use related texts and literature to teach the themes and integrate them into other content areas. Themes help children remember lesson content and help you make the most of each day.

T is for . . .

Tic-Tac-Know

Prepare a list of nine questions on a current area of study. Draw a Tic-Tac-Toe grid on the chalkboard, and write each number from 1 to 9 in a box in any order. Divide the class into two teams—the Xs and Os. Invite a volunteer from the X team to choose a box on the grid. Ask the question that corresponds with the number in that box. If the volunteer answers correctly, encourage him or her to write an X in that box. Then, invite a volunteer from the O team to do the same. The team with three Xs or three Os in a row wins as in regular Tic-Tac-Toe.

Tiles

Tiles from a home improvement store are not only great math manipulatives but are also useful for fostering literacy skills. Use tiles for the following activities:

● Write a number or operation sign on each tile. Invite children to work in pairs to design and solve each other's equations.
● Use permanent markers to write capital and lowercase letters for matching and spelling. Write a word on each tile, and have children create "super sentences" or sort words by parts of speech.

Tin Cans

Use tin cans to store materials for centers or other areas of the classroom. Have children bring cans from home, and ask the cafeteria to save gallon cans for you. Smooth out the sharp edges, and paint or cover them with contact paper. The gallon cans make great mobile centers for holding manipulatives, paper, and activity directions.

T is for...

Tongue Depressors

Here is one way to avoid long lines or waving hands during quiet writing. Assign each child a number and write it on a tongue depressor. Label a can *HELP*. Have children put their tongue depressor in the can when they need help.

Trays

Trays are a terrific way to define work areas and create boundaries for center activities. Children can also solve jigsaw puzzles and use math manipulatives on them. Organize materials on trays, and place them anywhere in the room for children to work on. Look for trays at fast food restaurants, the school cafeteria, or a restaurant supply store.

Tubs

Bathtubs have been and continue to be inviting places for children to "sink" into good books. They make a great addition to your reading center. Be on the lookout!

A Word of Advice

TEACH, TRANSFER

People seldom improve when they have no model to copy but themselves. —Anonymous

In the natural progression of teaching, demonstrating, and modeling new skills and concepts,
use materials that you can transfer to learning centers without modification.
Children practice and apply skills and concepts without a lot of explanation because they are already familiar with them.

U is for...

Umbrellas

The tiny umbrellas that come in tropical fruit drinks are perfect for patterning or showing fact families. Stick the umbrella "handles" in a piece of craft foam and you have an instant math activity.

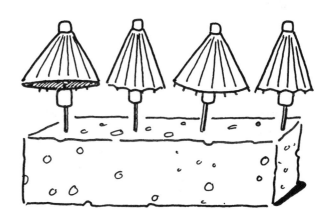

Unifix Cubes

Unifix cubes are a unique way to evaluate children. Try them in one of these ways:

- Give each child two colors of cubes, one light and one dark. Tell children the light colors represent answer A and the dark colors represent answer B. As you ask children questions, have them add the appropriate block to the answer stack. Visually scan for children's answers! This is a fun and quick way to review.
- To use Unifix cubes as a class management tool, give each child three cubes at the beginning of the day. If a child breaks a class rule, he or she must give you one of the cubes. If all three are lost before the day ends, the child receives a previously agreed upon consequence.

U.S. Maps

Maps make great puzzles. Laminate maps, and cut them up randomly, or by state or region. Place these puzzles in a social studies or geography center. For a quick language activity to do with maps, give each small group a U.S. map and a piece of lined paper. Set a timer, and ask each group to choose ten place-names and list them in alphabetical order.

A Word of Advice

UNDERACHIEVERS

Children who are treated as if they are uneducable almost invariably become uneducable. —Kenneth Clark

When children think they can you are halfway there. Set children up to be successful.
Don't look at last year's records until after the first nine weeks.
Assume all children in your classroom are gifted and they will be . . . each in his or her own way.

V is for...

Very Important Person

Recognize each child as a very important person in your classroom by giving your children an opportunity to tell about themselves and their families. The very first V.I.P. in your classroom should be you! Create a poster about you that includes your family, hobbies (if teaching isn't it), and pictures of yourself in the grade you are teaching. You might even be able to include schoolwork you did when in the same grade as your students. The children love this; it makes you real to them and helps strengthen that personal connection that is so important.

Vinyl

Vinyl is available at most fabric stores and comes in a variety of colors. Cut vinyl into the same size strip you would cut construction paper for making paper chains. Add Velcro to the ends, and you have a wonderful patterning activity for your math center. Have children record and label the patterns they made with the vinyl strips.

Visors

Make your own visors for a writing center using the Writer's Visor reproducible (page 76). Label the visors *Thinking, Creating, Writing, Editing,* and *Publishing* (or whatever is appropriate for your classroom). Color-code the visors so that all the visors for one job are the same color. As you work with a small group, you can see at a glance what a child is doing at the writing center. When you take a walk around the room to observe, monitor, and evaluate, you know exactly what to look for.

Vocabulary Bookmarks

Vocabulary bookmarks are a great way for children to record new words and keep their spot in their book at the same time. Use the Vocabulary Bookmarks reproducible (page 77). Have children use their bookmark as they begin reading a new book. Have children pause in their reading to write words on their bookmark. Have children search for nouns, proper nouns, verbs, new words, words with two syllables, blends, and more!

A Word of Advice

VACATIONS

To do great work a man must be very idle as well as very industrious. —Samuel Butler

We have all experienced "borderline" burnout! Remember, you can't burn out if you haven't been on fire!
Be good to yourself, take time for yourself, and you will be a better teacher, a better colleague, and a better human being.

W is for . . .

WetSet™

WetSet is a great product by Crayola®. Children use the clay to make their projects, and then they place the clay in water to set it. No heat is required. Children can make pots, beads, animals, bugs, and more. The clay comes in a variety of colors and can be painted.

Wheelbarrows and Wagons

Wheelbarrows and wagons make great centers. Use them to store materials and "wheel" them to different areas of the classroom. Metal ones also make terrific magnetic "boards."

Wikki Stix

Wikki Stix are colored strings coated with wax. Invite your children to use them to make letters, words, shapes, numbers, states, land forms, the digestive system, and more. Have children complete their work on a place mat. When they are done, demonstrate how to use a piece of white paper and crayons to preserve their work. Have children place paper over their sculpture, and show them how to use the side of the crayon to make a rubbing of it. To avoid tangling the Wikki Stix, divide a solid-color place mat into enough columns for each color of Wikki Stix. Have children sort the stix to be ready for the next child.

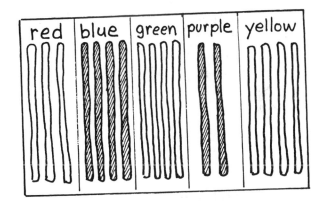

Windows

Use the windows in your classroom to maximize limited display area! Purchase suction cups with hooks, and stick them to the windows. Attach directions, examples, pocket charts, and menus to the hooks for an instant display area.

W is for . . .

Winter Picnics

February is the halfway point of winter, and a white winter picnic is a nice way to take a "day off" from the season. Have each child bring an all-white lunch (e.g., turkey on white bread with mayonnaise, popcorn, cauliflower, and milk). Place white sheets on the floor for children to picnic on. Make white cupcakes with white icing sprinkled with coconut as a special treat.

Word Banks

Word banks are a wonderful way for children to collect words as they learn to read and write. The problem has always been how to organize the words so children can find them! Ask each child to bring from home a 3" x 5" (7.5 cm x 12.5 cm) file box, index cards, and alphabet dividers. Each day have children add at least one word to their word bank by having them draw a picture on a card and write the word correctly. Then, have children file the card behind the appropriate letter in their file box. This makes it very easy for children to retrieve the words when they need them! Word banks are also great for alphabetical order and alliteration activities. Have children keep the boxes at their desk. Yes, sometimes they do fall off, but as children pick the cards up, they are practicing alphabetical order!

Write the Room

Write the Room is another simple and effective center for your classroom. Provide two or three children with clipboards, paper, and a pencil. Have children walk around the room and write down words to add to their word banks or record specific kinds of words that you are currently studying or reviewing (e.g., nouns, verbs, long and short vowel words, blends, and compound words).

A Word of Advice

WORK

Nothing is particularly hard if you divide it into small jobs. —Booker T. Washington

This applies to children and teachers.
When teachers are overwhelmed with the task at hand they will use adult "avoidance" techniques.
You might clean off your desk, organize materials, or make those phone calls you have been dreading.
Children will do the same thing. Children will avoid their overwhelming task
by looking at the end of a pencil or talking to a classmate. Help children break tasks down into manageable portions.

X is for . . .

Xocoatl

Xocoatl is the Aztec word for chocolate. Everyone loves chocolate. Use chocolate as a topic for a research project and to have children explore solids and liquids, graph, sort, make patterns, measure, and more. Have children bring in their favorite miniatures for math activities, and keep the rest for a chocolate fix throughout the year. Some days only require one piece at the end of the day and other days require a whole package. You be the judge!

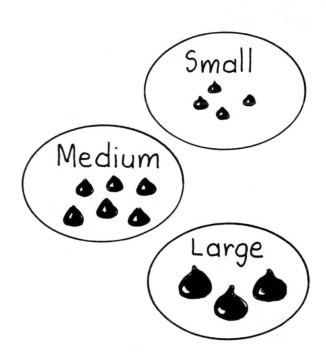

Xylophones

These musical instruments are a tried and true way to give children signals to quiet down, clean up, or move to a transitional activity. Get one cheaply at a toy store, but try it out before taking it home. Some are more in tune than others.

A Word of Advice

EXAMPLE

Teachers teach more by what they are than by what they say. —Anonymous

Children are always watching every move you make,
everything you say, and the way you say it!
Use this to your advantage.
Be an eXample.

Y is for . . .

Yarn

Yarn is useful for displaying children's work and tying together class books and a multitude of art projects, so be sure to have a few skeins on hand at all times. Try these yarn uses:

- Have children make "yarn books." Have children write and illustrate a story on several index cards, hole-punch the top of each, and string the cards together to tell a story.
- Send a piece of yarn home over a long weekend, and have children save items that represent what they did by tying them on the yarn. Each child will return to school with a "yarn" to tell about his or her weekend.
- Make an instant picture frame by wrapping yarn around pins placed in the four corners of a child's work.

Year's End

Have each child wear or bring a plain white T-shirt to school. Provide children with colored permanent markers, and invite them to sign each other's shirts. Wear a pair of white tennis shoes, and invite your children to sign your shoes. Use fabric paints to add a border around the top of the rubber sole, and wear the shoes for special occasions throughout the following years.

A Word of Advice

YOU

A teacher affects eternity; he can never tell where his influence stops. —Henry Adams

You impact and influence children every single moment of every day.
You make the difference.

Z is for . . .

Zone

A zone is an area with a specified use. Make your classroom a "learning" zone. Check the following specifications for your classroom:

● Are you building a classroom community?
● Do you teach to all levels and learning styles represented in your classroom?
● Does your classroom provide a "comfort" zone for both children and adults?

A Word of Advice

ZEAL

Hide not your talents. They for use were made. What's a sundial in the shade? —Ben Franklin

Show the intense enthusiasm you have for what you create in your classroom.
When you are enthusiastic about what you provide, children are enthusiastic about receiving it.
Enjoy your children. Enjoy teaching and creating a learning environment.

Names_____ Date_____

ABC Ideas

Page 1

	Book One_____ (title)	Book Two_____ (title)
A		
B		
C		
D		
E		
F		
G		
H		
I		

ABC Ideas

Page 2

	Book One_____ (title)	Book Two_____ (title)
J		
K		
L		
M		
N		
O		
P		
Q		
R		

ABC Ideas

Page 3

	Book One_____ (title)	Book Two_____ (title)
S		
T		
U		
V		
W		
X		
Y		
Z		

Colors

Directions: Color the mice to show how you made orange, green, and purple clay.

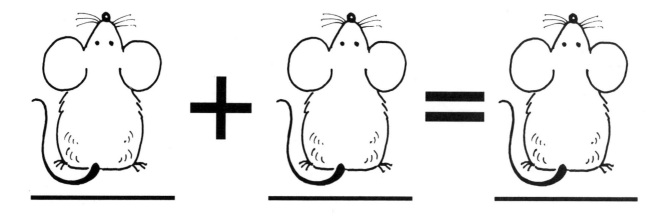

Hands

Teachin' Smart © 1999 Creative Teaching Press

Dog-Bone Math

Domino Math

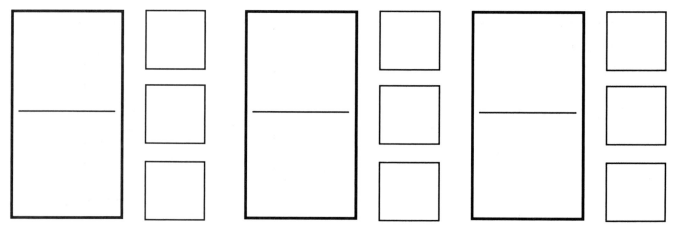

Magic Squares

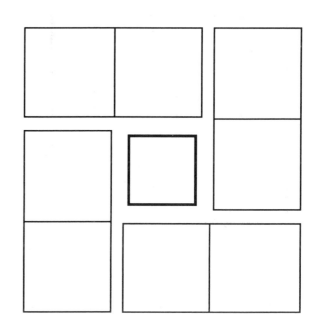

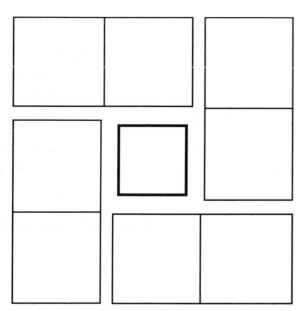

Domino Fractions

1/2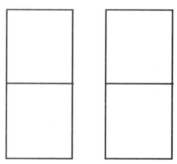

1/3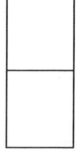

2/3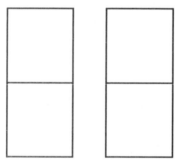

1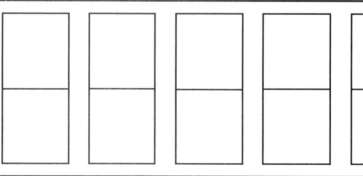

Name _____

Date _____

Jelly-Bean Graph

Directions:
1. Choose an egg.
2. Open the egg and sort the jelly beans by color.
3. Place the jelly beans on the graph. Color in the square under each jelly bean with that color.

red	green	orange	black	purple	pink	yellow

Directions:
Fill in each blank with the number of jelly beans you have.

I have

_____ red jelly beans.

_____ green jelly beans.

_____ orange jelly beans.

_____ black jelly beans.

_____ purple jelly beans.

_____ pink jelly beans.

_____ yellow jelly beans.

Jelly-Bean Money

Jelly Beans

Name _____

Date _____

_____ × $_____ = $_____

_____ × $_____ = $_____

_____ × $_____ = $_____

_____ × $_____ = $_____

_____ × $_____ = $_____

_____ × $_____ = $_____

_____ × $_____ = $_____

How much are all the
jelly beans worth? $_____

Jelly Beans

Name _____

Date _____

_____ × $_____ = $_____

_____ × $_____ = $_____

_____ × $_____ = $_____

_____ × $_____ = $_____

_____ × $_____ = $_____

_____ × $_____ = $_____

_____ × $_____ = $_____

How much are all the
jelly beans worth? $_____

Class List

Writer's Visor

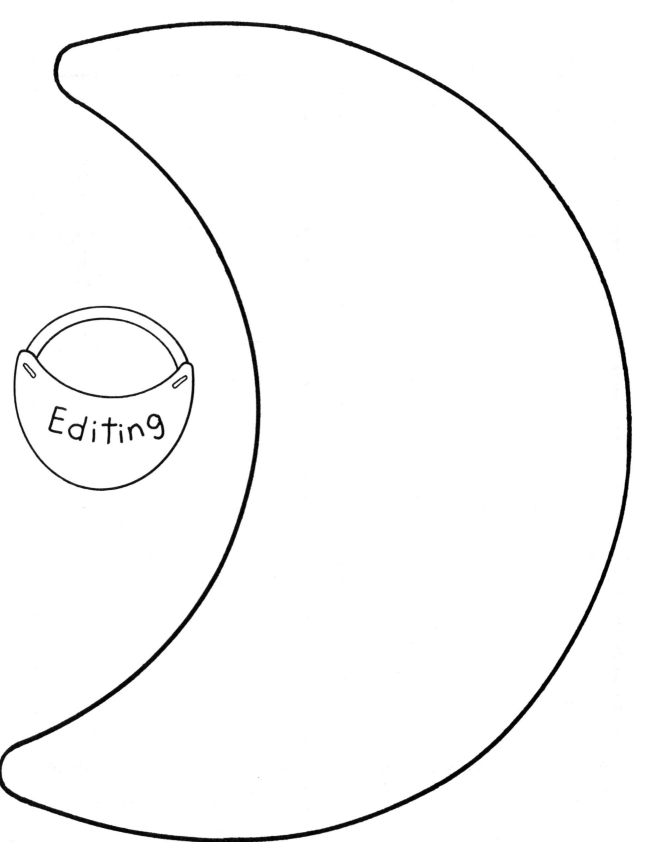

Editing

Vocabulary Bookmarks

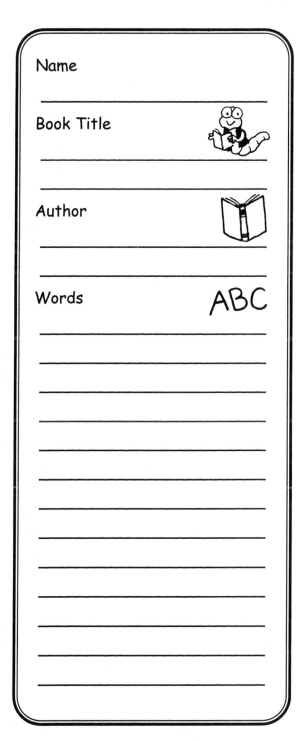

Name
_____

Book Title
_____
_____

Author
_____
_____

Words   ABC
_____
_____
_____
_____
_____
_____
_____
_____
_____
_____
_____
_____

Name
_____

Book Title
_____
_____

Author
_____
_____

Words   ABC
_____
_____
_____
_____
_____
_____
_____
_____
_____
_____
_____
_____

Index . . .

ABC Order
Alphabetical Order	6
Blocks	8
Calendar Shapes	11
Cereal Boxes	12
Paper-Cup Stacks and Lines	41
Seed Packets	50
Stamping Kits	51
Stringing Blocks	52
Word Banks	60

Art and Drama
Balloons	7
Clay Colors	13
Colorful Art	14
Fabric	19
Garland	22
Instant Programs	26
Jewelry	28
Jigsaw Puzzle Pieces	28
Noodles	38
WetSet™	59
Yarn	62

Behavior
Raffle	47
Rules	49
Unifix Cubes	57

Celebrations/Themes
Birthdays	8
Border Fun	9
Flags and Banners	20
Hobby Hall	25
Instant Programs	26
Ketchup Week	30
Lunch	34
Magic Spray	35
Name Necklaces	37
Themes	54
Very Important Person	58
Winter Picnics	60
Year's End	62

Center Organization
Aprons	6
Bookmarks	9
Chalkboard Paint	12
Dating	15
Fabric	19
Luggage	33
Overalls	40
Picnic-Basket Center	42
Tackle Boxes	53
Tents	54
Tin Cans	55
Trays	56
Tubs	56
Wheelbarrows and Wagons	59

Giving Directions
Albums	5
Cereal Boxes	12
Clipboards	13
Disk Holders	15
Easels	17
Erasers	18
Horizontal Picture Holders	25
Menus	36
Napkin Rings	37
Overalls	40
Project Boards	44
Question Quilts	45
Tin Cans	55
Windows	59

Language: Manipulatives
Barrettes	8
Border Fun	9
Calendar Shapes	11
Ice Cube Trays	26
Letter Sorts	32
Lima Beans	33
Magnetic Manipulatives	35
Metal Pails	36
Noodles	38
Seed Packets	50
Stamping Kits	51
Tiles	55
Wikki Stix	59

Language: Structure
Alliteration Arranging	5
Big Book "Pockets"	8
Blocks	8
Buttons	10
Calendar Pictures	11
Calendar Shapes	11
Cereal Boxes	12
Color Coding	14
Flyswatters	21
Letter Sorts	32
Newspapers	37
Questions and Answers	45
Quotation Marks	46
Rocks	47
Stringing Blocks	52
Tiles	55
U.S. Maps	57
Vocabulary Bookmarks	58
Write the Room	60

Making Books
Fabric	19
Fold and Crease	21
Paper-Plate Book Covers	41
Place Mats	42
Pringles®-Can Tales	43
Rubber Bands	48
Rulers	49
Yarn	62

Making Learning Fun
Gift Game	22
Glasses	22
Hats	25
Overhead Projectors	40

Pointers · 43
Quill Pens · 46
Round-Robin Sharing · 48
Sewing Cards · 50
Shaving Cream · 50
Stuffed Animals · 52
Tic-Tac-Know · 55
Tubs · 56
Yarn · 62

Math: Computation and Graphing
Balls · 7
Bottled Ink Bingo Markers · 10
Candy · 12
Colorful Art · 14
Dominos · 16
Eggs · 17
Fabric · 19
Paper-Cup Stacks and Lines · 41
Smiles · 51
Xocoatl · 61

Math: Manipulatives
Border Fun · 9
Buttons · 10
Calendar Shapes · 11
Dog Bones · 16
Eggs · 17
Garland · 22
Ice Cube Trays · 26
Jewelry · 28
Jigsaw Puzzle Pieces · 28
Lima Beans · 33
Magnetic Manipulatives · 35
Metal Pails · 36
Noodles · 38
Nuts · 38
Rocks · 47
Silverware · 51
Stamping Kits · 51
Trays · 56
Wikki Stix · 59
Xocoatl · 61

Math: Numbers and Numerical Value
Balls · 7
Candy · 12
Marshmallow Number Stands · 35
Paper-Cup Stacks and Lines · 41
Tiles · 55
Xocoatl · 61

Organizing Materials
Calculators · 11
Clothes Hangers with Clips · 13
Divided Boxes · 15
Envelopes · 18
Jars · 28
Key Rack · 31
Odds and Ends · 39
Pencil Boxes · 41
Shoe Boxes and Bags · 51

Patterning, Sequencing, and Sorting
Barrettes · 8
Border Fun · 9
Bottled Ink Bingo Markers · 10
Buttons · 10
Candy · 12
Dog Bones · 16
Eggs · 17
Kabob Cooking · 30
Kool-Aid® Packages · 31
Noodles · 38
Seed Packets · 50
Umbrellas · 57
Vinyl · 58

Planning and Assessment
File Folders · 20
Master Planning · 36
Note Necklaces · 38
Seating Charts · 50
Unifix Cubes · 57

Responding to Literature
ABC Book Graphic Organizer · 5
Balloons · 7
Book Talk · 9
Clay Colors · 13
Guest Reader · 24
Instant Programs · 26
Jump Ropes · 29
Letter Writing · 32
Overhead Projectors · 40
Pillowcase Book Record · 42
Tape Recorders · 54

Science
After-Christmas Tree · 5
Journals · 29
Nests · 37
Wikki Stix · 59

Social Studies
Interesting Information · 27
Unifix Cubes · 57
Wikki Stix · 59

Tips for Teachers
Baby Wipes · 7
Fold and Crease · 21
Glue · 23
Hallway · 25
Ideas · 26
Lumberyards · 34
Outrageous Outfits · 39
Print Shops · 44
Restaurant Supply Store · 47
Tables · 53
Themes · 54
Tongue Depressors · 56
Visors · 58
Xylophones · 61
Zone · 63

Index...

Using Familiar Things in New Ways

Calculators	11
Crazy Containers	14
Do-It-Yourself Dry Erase Boards	15
Egg Cartons	17
Envelopes	18
Fabric	19
File Cabinet	19
Horizontal Picture Holders	25
Hula Hoops	25
Interactive Charts	27
Jars	28
Lazy Susans	32
Luggage	33
Overalls	40
Pocket Chart	43
Shoe Boxes and Bags	51
Swimming Pools	52
Tackle Boxes	53

Vocabulary and Spelling

Big Book "Pockets"	8
Calendar Shapes	11
File Folders	20
Flashlights	20
Key Chains	30
Lima Beans	33
Magic Tree	35
Paper-Cup Stacks and Lines	41
Read the Room	47
Shaving Cream	50
Stringing Blocks	52
Tiles	55
Vocabulary Bookmarks	58
Word Banks	60

Writing

Buttons	10
Calendar Pictures	11
Candy	12
Greeting Cards	23
Journals	29
Letter Writing	32
Luggage	33
Nests	37
Paper-Plate Book Covers	41
Picnic-Basket Center	42
Place Mats	42
Poetry	43
Pringles®-Can Tales	43
Questions and Answers	45
Rocks	47
Rubber Bands	48
Rulers	49
Stamping Kits	51
Tall Tales	53
Tongue Depressors	56
Yarn	62